MW01110415

JOY

JOY

Warren W. Wiersbe

VICTOR BOOKS

A DIVISION OF SCRIPTURE PRESS PUBLICATIONS INC.
USA CANADA ENGLAND

Copyediting: Afton Rorvik
Cover Design: Grace K. Chan Mallette

Library of Congress Cataloging-in-Publication Data

Wiersbe, Warren W.
    Joy / Warren W. Wiersbe.
       p.   cm.
    Each devotional is adapted from a chapter in: Be joyful. 1974.
    1. Bible N.T. Philippians—Devotional literature.
  2. Devotional calendars. I. Wiersbe, Warren W. Be joyful.
  II. Title.
  BS2705.4.W54   1994
  242'.2—dc20
                                      94-7625
                                         CIP

1 2 3 4 5 6 7 8 9 10 Printing/Year 98 97 96 95 94

If you are studying *Be Joyful* in a Sunday School class or small group, this 30-Day Devotional will complement your study. Each devotional is adapted from a chapter in *Be Joyful*. The following chart indicates the correlation. You may, of course, use this book without reference to *Be Joyful*.

Be Joyful	**Joy**
Book Chapter	**30-Day Devotional**
1	**Days 1 and 8**
2	**Days 2, 3, and 4**
3	**Days 5, 6, and 7**
4	**Days 9 and 10**
5	**Days 11, 12, and 13**
6	**Days 14 and 15**
7	**Days 16 and 17**
8	**Days 18, 19, and 20**
9	**Days 21, 22, and 23**
10	**Days 24 and 25**
11	**Days 26, 27, and 28**
12	**Days 29 and 30**

INTRODUCTION

The world uses the word *happiness*, but God talks about *joy*. There's a difference; and when you learn what that difference is, your life will be different.

Happiness depends on happenings, what goes on around you. When your plans work out right, when you feel good, when problems are at a minimum, then you're happy. But when you wake up with a headache, or the boss rearranges your schedule, or somebody you love is hurting, then that happiness fades; and you're left feeling discouraged and defeated. You feel like quitting.

But life doesn't have to be like that. You can substitute joy for happiness and experience a whole new kind of life.

Joy doesn't depend on what goes on *around* you. It depends on what goes on *within* you. It is the result of a right relationship with God, a right attitude toward life, and a right faith in the power of Christ. Happiness says, "I am the captain of my fate!" and courts disaster. Joy says, "I can do everything through Him who gives me strength" (Phil. 4:13) and marches to victory.

Paul didn't write the Epistle to the Philippians from a comfortable library or an ivory tower. When he wrote it, he was a prisoner in Rome *and in danger of being executed any day.* Yet this letter is saturated with joy and rejoicing. Why? Because Paul was a man who knew Christ, a single-minded man with a mission to fulfill and a God to serve.

Outlook helps to determine *outcome*; and in this letter, Paul tells you how to have the kind of outlook that produces joy. He shares the "open secret" of having joy in spite of circumstances, people, things, or worry. He explains the basic principles of Christian experience that can turn your life into a daily celebration of the joy of the Lord.

Yes, you'll still have problems and battles and burdens; but you'll find yourself overcoming instead of being overcome.

You'll find yourself joyfully saying with Paul, "I can do everything through Him who gives me strength."

—Warren W. Wiersbe

My thanks to Stan Campbell,
who compiled the contents of this book
and added thought-provoking questions
to enrich your personal growth.

*Read **Philippians 1:1-5***

The Secret of Joy

....

Paul's letter to the Philippian church is something of a missionary thank-you letter, but it is much more than that. It is the sharing of Paul's secret of Christian joy. At least 19 times in these four chapters, Paul mentions joy, rejoicing, or gladness!

The unusual thing about the letter is this: Paul's situation was such that there appeared to be no reason for him to be rejoicing. He was a Roman prisoner and his case was coming up shortly. He might be acquitted, or he might be beheaded! And, unfortunately, the believers at Rome (where he was being held) were divided: some were for Paul and some were against him. In fact, some of the Christians even wanted to make things more difficult for the apostle!

Yet, in spite of his danger and discomfort, Paul overflowed with joy. The secret of Christian joy is found in the way the believer thinks — his attitudes. After all, outlook determines outcome. As we think, so we are (Prov. 23:7).

Philippians, then, is a Christian psychology book, based solidly on biblical doctrine. It is a book that

> *"I thank my God every time I remember you.*
> *In all my prayers for all of you, I always*
> *pray with joy because of your partnership in*
> *the Gospel from the first day until now"*
> *(Philippians 1:3-5).*

....

explains the mind the believer must have if he is going to experience Christian joy in a world filled with trouble.

Applying God's Truth:

1. Can you recall a time or times when you experienced joy even under threatening or adverse situations?

2. What are some current situations that tend to keep you from experiencing joy? How might you keep from letting such situations rob you of joy?

3. As you go through these devotional readings, what are some thing you hope to accomplish?

Read **Philippians 1:6-7**

Reducing Friction

....

Isn't it remarkable that Paul is thinking of others and not of himself? As he awaits his trial in Rome, Paul's mind goes back to the believers in Philippi, and every recollection he has brings him joy. Read Acts 16; you may discover that some things happened to Paul at Philippi, the memory of which could produce sorrow. He was illegally arrested and beaten, was placed in the stocks, and was humiliated before the people. But even those memories brought joy to Paul. It was a source of joy to Paul to know that God was still working in the lives of his fellow-believers in Philippi. The basis for joyful Christian fellowship is to have God at work in our lives day by day.

"There seems to be friction in our home," a concerned wife said to a marriage counselor. "I really don't know what the trouble is."

"Friction is caused by one of two things," said the counselor, and to illustrate he picked up two blocks of wood from his desk. "If one block is moving and one is standing still, there's friction. Or, if both are moving but in opposite directions, there's friction. Now, which is it?"

"Being confident of this, that He who began a good work in you will carry it on to completion until the day of Christ Jesus"
(Philippians 1:6).

....

"I'll have to admit that I've been going backward in my Christian life, and Joe has really been growing," the wife admitted. "What I need is to get back to fellowship with the Lord."

Applying God's Truth:

1. Does your spiritual growth seem to be an occasional thing, or do you see it as an ongoing process with God in control? Explain.

2. What are some of the things that cause friction in your spiritual development?

3. When did God begin a good work in you? How has your life changed since that time? What additional changes do you anticipate?

Read *Philippians 1:8-10*

A Mark of Maturity

....

Paul found joy in his memories of the friends at Philippi and in his growing love for them. He also found joy in remembering them before the throne of grace in prayer. This is a prayer for maturity, and Paul begins with *love*. After all, if our Christian love is what it ought to be, everything else should follow. He prays that they might experience *abounding* love and *discerning* love. Christian love is not blind! The heart and mind work together so that we have discerning love and loving discernment. Paul wants his friends to grow in discernment.

The ability to distinguish is a mark of maturity. When a baby learns to speak, it may call every four-legged animal a "bow-wow." But then the child discovers that there are cats, dogs, white mice, cows, and other four-legged creatures. To a little child, one automobile is just like another, but not to a car-crazy teenager. He can spot the differences between models faster than his parents can even name the cars!

One of the sure marks of maturity is discerning love.

"This is my prayer: that your love may abound more and more in knowledge and depth of insight, so that you may be able to discern what is best and may be pure and blameless until the day of Christ"
(Philippians 1:9-10).

....

Applying God's Truth:

1. Think of ten close friends. How frequently do you pray for each one of them?

2. What do you think it means to have "discerning love"? In what ways is your love for others a discerning kind of love?

3. In your life do you seek what is good, or do you try to discern what is truly *best* for you?

Read **Philippians 1:11**

Fruitfulness vs. Busyness

....

The difference between spiritual fruit and human "religious activity" is that the fruit brings glory to Jesus Christ. Whenever we do anything in our own strength, we have a tendency to boast about it. True spiritual fruit is so beautiful and wonderful that no man can claim credit for it; the glory must go to God alone. This, then, is true Christian fellowship—a having-in-common that is much deeper than mere friendship.

Jerry had to go to New York City for special surgery, and he hated to go. "Why can't we have it done at home?" he asked his doctor. "I don't know a soul in that big, unfriendly city!" But when he and his wife arrived at the hospital, there was a pastor to meet them and invite them to stay at his home until they got settled. The operation was serious, and the wait in the hospital was long and difficult; but the fellowship of the pastor and his wife brought a new joy to Jerry and his wife. They learned that circumstances need not rob us of joy if we will but permit these circumstances to strengthen the fellowship of the Gospel.

*"Filled with the fruit of righteousness
that comes through Jesus Christ — to the
glory and praise of God"*
(Philippians 1:11).

....

Applying God's Truth:

1. What are some characteristics you would consider "the fruit of righteousness"?

2. In contrast, what are some of the things you would classify as only "religious activity"?

3. In which of your relationships would you say you experience genuine Christian fellowship? In which ones do you settle for "mere friendship"?

Read **Philippians 1:12-13**

Onward, Pioneers

Everyone has heard of Charles Haddon Spurgeon the famous British preacher, but few know the story of his wife, Susannah. Early in their married life, Mrs. Spurgeon became an invalid. It looked as though her only ministry would be encouraging her husband and praying for his work. But God gave her a burden to share her husband's books with pastors who were unable to purchase them. This burden soon led to the founding of the "Book Fund." As a work of faith, the "Book Fund" provided thousands of pastor with tools for their work. All this was supervised by Mrs. Spurgeon from her home. It was a pioneer ministry.

God still wants His children to take the Gospel into new areas. He wants us to be pioneers, and sometimes He arranges circumstances so that we can be nothing else but pioneers. In fact, that is how the Gospel originally came to Philippi! Paul had tried to enter other territory, but God had repeatedly shut the door (Acts 16:6-10). Paul wanted to take the message eastward into Asia, but God directed him to take it westward into Europe. What a difference it would have made in the history of mankind if Paul had been permitted to follow his plan!

"It has become clear throughout the whole palace guard and to everyone else that I am in chains for Christ"
(Philippians 1:13).

....

Applying God's Truth:

1. Who are some people you know who aren't in prominent leadership roles, yet who have a lot of impact on others for advancing the Gospel? What can you learn from such people?

2. What are some "new areas" where you might be able to carry the Gospel?

3. Envision yourself as a spiritual "pioneer." What are some of the potential risks you need to be aware of? What are some of the potential benefits?

Read **Philippians 1:14-17**

Chains and Change

....

Sometimes God has to put "chains" on His people to get them to accomplish a "pioneer advance" that could never happen any other way. Young mothers may feel chained to the home as they care for their children, but God can use those "chains" to reach people with the message of salvation. Susannah Wesley was the mother of 19 children, before the days of labor-saving devices and disposable diapers! Out of that large family came John and Charles Wesley, whose combined ministries shook the British Isles.

At six weeks of age, Fanny Crosby was blinded, but even as a youngster she determined not to be confined by the chains of darkness. In time, she became a mighty force for God through her hymns and Gospel songs.

The secret is this: when you have the single mind (see Day 8), you look upon your circumstances as God-given opportunities for the furtherance of the Gospel, and you rejoice at *what God is going to do* instead of complaining about *what God did not do*.

*"Because of my chains, most of the
brothers in the Lord have been
encouraged to speak the Word of God
more courageously and fearlessly"*
(Philippians 1:14).

....

Applying God's Truth:

1. What are some ways in which you feel "chained"?

2. Do you have any regrets — or perhaps
   complaints — of times when you hoped God would
   work in a certain way, yet He didn't?

3. What are some ways that you might overcome your
   chains and become a better witness for God?

   Just yield to God my whole life!

Read **Philippians 1:18-20**

Larger Than Life

....

Does Christ need to be magnified? After all, how can a mere human being ever magnify the Son of God? Well, the stars are much bigger than the telescope, and yet the telescope magnifies them and brings them closer. The believer's body is to be a telescope that brings Jesus Christ close to people. To the average person, Christ is a misty figure in history who lived centuries ago. But as the unsaved watch the believer go through a crisis, they can see Jesus magnified and brought so much closer. To the Christian with the single mind (see Day 8), Christ is with us here and now.

The telescope brings distant things closer, and the microscope makes tiny things look big. To the unbeliever, Jesus is not very big. Other people and other things are far more important. But as the unbeliever watches the Christian go through a crisis experience, he ought to be able to see how big Jesus Christ really is. The believer's body is a "lens" that makes a "little Christ" look very big, and a "distant Christ" come very close.

Paul was not afraid of life or death! Either way, he wanted to magnify Christ in his body. No wonder he had joy!

*"I eagerly expect and hope that I will in no way
be ashamed, but will have sufficient courage
so that now as always Christ will be exalted in
my body, whether by life or by death"*
(Philippians 1:20).

....

Applying God's Truth:

1. Can you think of any recent ways in which you have magnified (exalted) God? If so, how?

2. Do you ever feel embarrassed when presenting the Gospel to others? How do you muster "sufficient courage" to maintain an effective personal ministry?

3. What kind of "lens" do you provide through which friends and acquaintances see Christ? Do you magnify Him or tend to obscure the view in some way?

8

Read **Philippians 1:21-24**

The Single Mind
....

James tells us that a double-minded man is unstable in all he does (James 1:8). Or, to use the old Latin proverb: "When the pilot does not know what port he is heading for, no wind is the right wind." The reason many Christians are upset by circumstances is because they do not cultivate "the single mind." Paul expresses this attitude of single-hearted devotion to Christ thus: "For to me, to live is Christ and to die is gain."

Paul discusses his difficult circumstances and faces them honestly. But his circumstances cannot rob him of his joy because he is not living to enjoy circumstances; he is living to serve Jesus Christ. He is a man with purpose. He did not look at Christ through his circumstances; rather, he looked at his circumstances through Christ—and this changed everything.

Paul rejoiced in his difficult circumstances because they helped to strengthen his fellowship with other Christians, gave him opportunity to lead others to Christ, and enabled him to defend the Gospel before the courts of Rome. When you have the single mind,

"To me, to live is Christ and to die is gain"
(Philippians 1:21).

....

your circumstances work *for* you and not *against* you.

Applying God's Truth:

1. What do you think it means to be "single minded," or to "have the single mind"?

2. What dominates your thoughts more than anything else?

3. Would you say your circumstances seem to influence your attitude about Jesus? Or does your relationship with Jesus tend to influence all your circumstances? Explain.

Read **Philippians 1:25-28**

People May Be Watching

....

My wife and I were visiting in London and one day decided to go to the zoo. We boarded the bus and sat back to enjoy the ride; but it was impossible to enjoy it because of the loud, coarse conversation of the passengers at the front of the bus. Unfortunately, they were Americans; and we could see the Britishers around us raising their eyebrows and shaking their heads, as though to say, "Oh, yes, they're from America!" We were embarrassed because we knew that these people did not really represent the best of American citizens.

Paul is suggesting that we Christians are the citizens of heaven, and while we are on earth we ought to behave like heaven's citizens. He brings this concept up again in 3:20. It would be a very meaningful expression to the people in Philippi because Philippi was a Roman colony, and its citizens were actually Roman citizens, protected by Roman law. The church of Jesus Christ is a colony of heaven on earth! And we ought to behave like the citizens of heaven.

....

*"Whatever happens, conduct yourselves in
a manner worthy of the Gospel of Christ"*
(Philippians 1:27).

....

Applying God's Truth:

1. Why do you think Paul introduces his command
   with the phrase, "Whatever happens"?

2. Are you ever embarrassed by God? Are you ever
   embarrassed by other Christians? What's the
   difference?

3. How does your conduct relate to your expressions
   of faith? Try to think of some specific examples.

Read **Philippians 1:29-30**

Brothers in Arms

....

Satan wants us to think we are alone in the battle, that our difficulties are unique, but such is not the case. Paul reminds the Philippians that he is going through the same difficulties they are experiencing hundreds of miles from Rome! A change in geography is usually no solution to spiritual problems because human nature is the same wherever you go, and the enemy is everywhere. Knowing that my fellow believers are also sharing in the battle is an encouragement for me to keep going and to pray for them as I pray for myself.

Actually, going through spiritual conflict is one way we have *to grow in Christ.* God gives us the strength we need to stand firm against the enemy, and this confidence is proof to him that he will lose and we are on the winning side. As we face the enemy and depend on the Lord, He gives us all that we need for the battle. When the enemy sees our God-given confidence, it makes him fear.

So, the single mind enables us to have joy in the midst of battle because it produces in us consistency, cooperation, and confidence. We experience the joy of "spiritual teamwork" as we strive together for the faith of the Gospel.

*"It has been granted to you on behalf of
Christ not only to believe on Him, but also to
suffer for Him"*
(Philippians 1:29).

....

Applying God's Truth:

1. War buddies grow particularly close because of the
   sufferings they share. Can you think of some past
   trials that drew you close to other people?

2. How does it make you feel during times of stress to
   know that others have suffered — and continue to
   suffer — in similar ways?

3. How can being "single minded" be an advantage
   during times of suffering?

Read **Philippians 2:1-6**

The Potential of Privileges

....

Certainly as God, Jesus Christ did not need anything! He had all the glory and praise of heaven. With the Father and the Spirit, He reigned over the universe. But verse 6 states an amazing fact: He did not consider His equality with God as "something to be grasped." Jesus did not think of Himself; He thought of others. His outlook (or attitude) was that of unselfish concern for others. This is "the mind of Christ," an attitude that says, "I cannot keep my privileges for myself, I must use them for others; and to do this, I will gladly lay them aside and pay whatever price is necessary."

A reporter was interviewing a successful job counselor who had placed hundreds of workers in their vocations quite happily. When asked the secret of his success, the man replied: "If you want to find out what a worker is really like, don't give him responsi-bilities—give him *privileges.* Most people can handle responsibilities if you pay them enough, but it takes a real leader to handle privileges. A leader will use his privileges to help others and build the organization; a lesser man will use privileges to promote himself." Jesus used His heavenly privileges for the sake of others—for *our* sake.

"Your attitude should be the same as that of Christ Jesus: Who, being in very nature God, did not consider equality with God something to be grasped"
(Philippians 2:5-6).

....

Applying God's Truth:

1. Do you ever wish for fame and recognition? What are some of your specific desires? What do you think motivates such dreams?

2. When you've worked hard to earn certain privileges, how hard do you try to hold on to them? Can you think of recent instances when you willingly gave up your hard-earned privileges to help out someone else?

3. What does it mean to you that Jesus "did not consider equality with God something to be grasped"?

Read **Philippians 2:7-8**

Choosing Servanthood

....

Thinking of "others" in an abstract sense only is insufficient; we must get down to the nitty-gritty of true service. Jesus thought of others *and became a servant!* When Christ was born at Bethlehem, He entered into a *permanent* union with humanity from which there could be no escape. He willingly humbled Himself that He might lift us up! Jesus did not pretend to be a servant; He was not an actor playing a role. *He actually was a servant!* This was the true expression of His innermost nature. He was the God-Man, deity and humanity united in one, and He came as a servant.

Have you noticed as you read the four Gospels that it is Jesus who serves others, not others who serve Jesus? He is at the beck and call of all kinds of people—fishermen, harlots, tax collectors, the sick, the sorrowing. In the Upper Room, when His disciples apparently refused to minister, Jesus arose, laid aside His outer garments, put on the long linen towel, and *washed their feet!* (John 13) He took the place of a menial slave! This was the submissive mind in action— and no wonder Jesus experienced such joy!

"But [Jesus] made Himself nothing, taking the very nature of a servant, being made in human likeness. And being found in appearance as a man, He humbled Himself and became obedient to death—even death on a cross!"
(Philippians 2:7-8)

....

Applying God's Truth:

1. Think of your acts of service to others. What percentage of them would you say are absolutely genuine? What percent might be considered "acting" or obligation?

2. What do you think was Jesus' secret to being such a good servant?

3. Do you believe there is a direct connection between serving others and receiving personal joy? Do your actions reflect your knowledge of this connection?

Read **Philippians 2:9-11**

A Submissive Mind

Our Lord's exaltation began with His resurrection. When men buried the body of Jesus, that was the last thing any human hands did to Him. From that point on, it was God who worked. Men had done their worst to the Savior, but God exalted Him and honored Him. Men gave Him names of ridicule and slander, but the Father gave Him a glorious name!

The person with the submissive mind, as he lives for others, must expect sacrifice and service; but in the end, it is going to lead to glory. Joseph suffered and served for 13 years; but then God exalted him and made him the second ruler of Egypt. David was anointed king when he was but a youth. He experienced years of hardship and suffering, but at the right time, God exalted him as king of Israel.

The joy of the submissive mind comes not only from helping others, and sharing in the fellowship of Christ's sufferings, but primarily from the knowledge that we are glorifying God. We are letting our light shine through our good works, and this glorifies the Father in heaven. We may not see the glory today, but we shall see it when Jesus comes and rewards His faithful servants.

> *"Therefore God exalted Him . . . that at the name of Jesus every knee should bow . . . and every tongue confess that Jesus Christ is Lord, to the glory of God the Father"*
>
> *(Philippians 2: 9-11).*

....

Applying God's Truth:

1. On a scale of 1 (least) to 10 (most), how impatient do you feel when you serve others and don't receive an immediate reward or acknowledgment?

2. Is it enough for you to know that God will reward your good works *eventually?* Or is it still hard to keep doing good for people who don't seem to appreciate it?

3. How can you stay focused on God's promised rewards and not so disappointed when your good deeds go unrecognized?

Read **Philippians 2:12-13**

A Spiritual "Workout"

....

"Work out your salvation" does not suggest "Work for your own salvation." To begin with, Paul is writing to people who are already "saints" (1:1), which means they have trusted Christ and have been set apart for Him. The verb "work out" carries the meaning of "work to full completion," such as working out a problem in mathematics. In Paul's day it was also used for "working a mine," that is, getting out of the mine all the valuable ore possible; or "working a field" so as to get the greatest harvest possible. The purpose God wants us to achieve is Christlikeness, "to be conformed to the likeness of His Son" (Rom. 8:29). There are problems in life, but God will help us to "work them out." Our lives have tremendous potential, like a mine or a field, and He wants to help us fulfill that potential.

The phrase "work out your own salvation" probably has reference particularly to the special problems in the church at Philippi; but the statement also applies to the individual Christian. We are not to be "cheap imitations" of other people, especially "great Christians." We are to follow only what we see of Christ in their lives!

*"Continue to work out your salvation with
fear and trembling, for it is God who works
in you to will and to act according to His
good purpose"*
(Philippians 2:12-13).

....

Applying God's Truth:

1. On a scale of 1 (least) to 10 (most), how hard would
   you say you try to "work out your own salvation"?

2. Does your relationship with God still involve a
   degree of "fear and trembling," or have you begun to
   take some of your spiritual privileges for granted?
   Explain.

3. List some ways that God has worked in your life
   during the past few months, and thank Him for
   each one.

*Read **Philippians 2:14-18***

Victory through Surrender

....

The world's philosophy is that joy comes from aggression: fight everybody to get what you want, and you will get it and be happy. The example of Jesus is proof enough that the world's philosophy is wrong. He never used a sword or any other weapon; yet He won the greatest battle in history — the battle against sin and death and hell. He defeated hatred by manifesting love; He overcame lies with truth. *Because He surrendered, He was victorious!*

There is a twofold joy that comes to the person who possesses and practices the submissive mind: a joy hereafter and a joy here and now. In the day of Christ, God is going to reward those who have been faithful to Him. The faithful Christian will discover that his sufferings on earth have been transformed into glory in heaven! He will see that his work was not in vain. It was this same kind of promise of future joy that helped our Savior in His sufferings on the cross (Heb. 12:1-2).

But we do not have to wait for the return of Christ to start experiencing the joy of the submissive mind. That joy is a present reality, and it comes through sacrifice and service.

*"Even if I am being poured out like a drink
offering on the sacrifice and service coming
from your faith, I am glad and rejoice with
all of you"*
(Philippians 2:7).

....

Applying God's Truth:

1. Do you ever experience joy because of submission
    to others? In what specific ways?

2. What are some of the here-and-now joys you
    experience on a regular basis? How might you
    increase this level of joy?

3. What are some future joys you look forward to?

Read **Philippians 2:20-21**

In Search of Good Samaritans

....

A reporter in San Bernardino, California arranged for a man to lie in the gutter on a busy street. Hundreds of people passed the man, but not one stopped to help him or even show sympathy!

Newspapers across the country a few years ago told how 38 people watched a man stalk a young lady and finally attack her — and none of the spectators even picked up a phone to call the police!

A Kentucky doctor was driving down the highway to visit a patient when he saw an accident take place. He stopped and gave aid to the injured and then made his visit. One of the drivers he helped sued him!

Is it possible to be a "Good Samaritan" today? Must everybody harden his heart in order to protect himself? Perhaps sacrifice and service are ancient virtues that somehow do not fit into our so-called modern civilization. It is worth noting that even in Paul's day mutual concern was not a popular virtue. The Christians at Rome were not too interested in the problems at Philippi; Paul could not find *one person* among them willing to go to Philippi. Times have not changed too much.

> *"I have no one else like [Timothy], who
> takes a genuine interest in your welfare.
> For everyone looks out for his own
> interests, not those of Jesus Christ"*
> *(Philippians 2:20-21).*

....

Applying God's Truth:

1. Try to recall one time when you needed help but no one was willing to assist you in any way. How did you feel?

2. What are some of the jobs in your church that are hardest to fill? Why do you think it's so tough to find volunteers for certain jobs?

3. What are some ways that people you know "look out for [their] own interests, not those of Jesus Christ"?

Read **Philippians 2:22-30**

A Servant's Reward

....

Timothy knew the meaning of sacrifice and service, but God rewarded him for his faithfulness. To begin with, Timothy had the joy of helping others. To be sure, there were hardships and difficulties, but there were also victories and blessings. He had the joy of serving with the great Apostle Paul and assisting him in some of his most difficult assignments.

But perhaps the greatest reward God gave to Timothy was to choose him to be Paul's replacement when the great apostle was called home. Paul himself wanted to go to Philippi, but had had to send Timothy in his place. But, what an honor! Timothy was not only Paul's "son," and Paul's servant, but he became Paul's substitute. His name is held in high regard by Christians today, something that young Timothy never dreamed of when he was busy serving Christ.

The submissive mind is not the product of an hour's sermon, or a week's seminar, or even a year's service. The submissive mind grows in us as, like Timothy, we yield to the Lord and seek to serve others.

"Timothy has proved himself, because as a son with his father he has served with me in the work of the Gospel. I hope, therefore, to send him as soon as I see how things go with me"
(Philippians 2:22-23).

....

Applying God's Truth:

1. Who is the person you know who best fits the description of Timothy given in this section?

2. Do you have anyone you can count on in the same way that Paul counted on Timothy? If not, how might you begin such a relationship with someone?

3. In the areas of your personal ministry, how are you training people to take your place when you move on to new places or other opportunities?

Read **Philippians 3:1-3**

No Confidence in the Flesh

....

The popular religious philosophy of today is, "The Lord helps those who help themselves." It was also popular in Paul's day, and it is just as wrong today as it was then. By "the flesh," Paul means "the old nature" that we received at birth. The Bible has nothing good to say about "flesh," and yet most people today depend entirely on what they themselves can do to please God. Flesh only corrupts God's way on earth. It profits nothing as far as spiritual life is concerned. It has nothing good in it. No wonder we should put no confidence in the flesh!

A lady was arguing with her pastor about this matter of faith and works. "I think that getting to heaven is like rowing a boat," she said. "One oar is faith, and the other is works. If you use both, you get there. If you use only one, you go around in circles."

"There is only one thing wrong with your illustration," replied the pastor. "Nobody is going to heaven *in a rowboat!*"

There is only one "good work" that takes the sinner to heaven: the finished work of Christ on the cross.

> *"It is we who are the circumcision, we who worship by the Spirit of God, who glory in Christ Jesus, and who put no confidence in the flesh"*
> *(Philippians 3:3).*

....

Applying God's Truth:

1. What are some ways that you have observed people "put confidence in the flesh"?

2. Create your own model (pie chart, graph, etc.) to indicate how you think faith and works are related.

3. In contrast to putting confidence in the flesh, what does it mean to "worship by the Spirit of God"?

Read **Philippians 3:4-7**

Measuring Sticks

....

Every Jew could boast of his own blood heritage. Some Jews could boast of their faithfulness to the Jewish religion. But Paul could boast of those things *plus* his zeal in persecuting the church. We might ask, "How could a sincere man like Saul of Tarsus be so wrong?" The answer is: *he was using the wrong measuring stick!*

Like the rich young ruler (Mark 10:17-22) and the Pharisee in Christ's parable (Luke 18:10-14), Saul of Tarsus was looking at the *outside* and not the *inside*. He was comparing himself with standards set by men, not by God. As far as obeying *outwardly* the demands of the Law, Paul was a success, but he did not stop to consider the *inward* sins he was committing. In the Sermon on the Mount, Jesus makes it clear that there are sinful *attitudes* and *appetites* as well as sinful *actions* (Matt. 5:21-48).

When he looked at himself or looked at others, Saul of Tarsus considered himself to be righteous. But one day he saw himself as compared with Jesus Christ! It was then that he changed his evaluations and values, and abandoned "works righteousness" for the righteousness of Jesus Christ.

*"If anyone else thinks he has reasons to put
confidence in the flesh, I have more. . . .
But whatever was to my profit I now
consider loss for the sake of Christ"*
(Philippians 3:4, 7).

....

Applying God's Truth:

1. Can you recall a time when you devoted a lot of time
    and energy to a project that didn't ultimately
    accomplish much? If so, how can you more
    effectively channel your efforts in the future?

2. Paul had worked very hard on his religion. Why do
    you think he was so quick to "consider [it] loss for
    the sake of Christ"?

3. Can you think of anything you might be clinging to
    that would be better to "consider loss" in order to
    continue to grow spiritually?

Read *Philippians 3:8-11*

Gaining and Losing

....

Remember Jim Elliot's words: "He is no fool to give what he cannot keep to gain what he cannot lose." This is what Paul experienced: he lost his religion and his reputation, but he gained far more than he lost. In fact, the gains were so thrilling that Paul considered all other things nothing but garbage in comparison!

No wonder he had joy — his life did not depend on the cheap things of the world but on the eternal values found in Christ. Paul had the "spiritual mind" and looked at the things of earth from heaven's point of view. People who live for things are never really happy because they must constantly protect their treasures and worry lest they lose their value. Not so the believer with the spiritual mind; his treasures in Christ can never be stolen and they never lose their value.

Maybe now is a good time for you to become an accountant and evaluate the things that matter most to you.

"I consider everything a loss compared to the surpassing greatness of knowing Christ Jesus my Lord, for whose sake I have lost all things. I consider them rubbish, that I may gain Christ"
(Philippians 3:8).

....

Applying God's Truth:

1. What is the single force that drives you more than any other?

2. What did you formerly value that you now consider "rubbish"? Why?

3. List the things you tend to value and contrast them with the eternal values made possible by Christ. Do your feelings toward your possessions tend to change? In what ways?

Read **Philippians 3:12-13a**

Beyond Compare
....

Harry came out of the manager's office with a look on his face dismal enough to wilt the roses on the secretary's desk.

"You didn't get fired?" she asked.

"No, it's not that bad. But he sure did lay into me about my sales record. I can't figure it out; for the past month I've been bringing in plenty of orders. I thought he'd compliment me, but instead he told me to get with it." Later in the day, the secretary talked to her boss about Harry. The boss chuckled. "Harry is one of our best salesmen and I'd hate to lose him. But he has a tendency to rest on his laurels and be satisfied with his performance. If I didn't get him mad at me once a month, he'd never produce!"

Many Christians are self-satisfied because they compare their "running" with that of other Christians, usually those who are not making much progress. Had Paul compared himself with others, he would have been tempted to be proud and perhaps to let up a bit. After all, there were not too many believers in Paul's day who had experienced all that he had! But Paul did

> *"I press on to take hold of that for which Christ Jesus took hold of me. Brothers, I do not consider myself yet to have taken hold of it"*
> *(Philippians 3:12-13a).*

....

not compare himself with others; he compared himself *with himself* and with *Jesus Christ!* The mature Christian honestly evaluates himself and strives to do better.

Applying God's Truth:

1. Do you think comparing yourself to others is always wrong? Why?

2. In a spiritual sense, can you identify any recent times when you may have tended to compare yourself to someone else rather than imitating the model Jesus has set?

3. When was the last time you tried to objectively evaluate your spiritual growth for the past month or year? How can you ensure that you don't "coast" too long without checking for progress?

Read **Philippians 3:13b-14**

Finding a Specialty

....

Before the tragedy of the Chicago fire in 1871, D. L. Moody was involved in Sunday School promotion, YMCA work, evangelistic meetings, and many other activities; but after the fire, he determined to devote himself exclusively to evangelism. "One thing I do" became a reality to him. As a result, millions of people heard the Gospel.

The believer must devote himself to "running the Christian race." No athlete succeeds by doing everything; he succeeds by *specializing*. There are those few athletes who seem proficient in many sports, but they are the exception. The winners are those who concentrate, who keep their eyes on the goal and let nothing distract them. They are devoted entirely to their calling. Like Nehemiah the wall-building governor, they reply to the distracting invitations, "I am carrying on a great project and cannot go down" (Neh. 6:3).

Concentration is the secret of power. If a river is allowed to overflow its banks, the area around it becomes a swamp. But if that river is dammed and controlled, it becomes a source of power. It is wholly a

> *"But one thing I do: Forgetting what is*
> *behind and straining toward what is ahead,*
> *I press on toward the goal to win the prize*
> *for which God has called me heavenward in*
> *Christ Jesus"*
> *(Philippians 3:13b-14).*

....

matter of values and priorities, living for that which
matters most.

Applying God's Truth:

1. In "running the Christian race," would you say you
    are better in the short sprints or the long distance
    runs?

2. What would you say is one area of ministry in which
    you could "specialize"?

3. Are you able to forget what is behind and press on
    toward the goal to win the prize? Or are certain
    events of your past weighing you down and
    impeding your progress?

Read *Philippians 3:15-16*

Rules of the Race

....

It is not enough to run hard and win the race; the runner must also obey the rules. In the Greek games, the judges were very strict about this. One day each Christian will stand before the judgment seat of Christ (Rom. 14:10-12). The Greek word for "judgment seat" is *bema,* the very same word used to describe the place where the Olympic judges gave out the prizes! If we have disciplined ourselves to obey the rules, we shall receive a prize.

Biblical history is filled with people who began the race with great success but failed at the end because they disregarded God's rules. They did not lose their salvation, but they did lose their rewards. It happened to Lot, Samson, Saul, and Ananias and Sapphira. And it can happen to us!

It is an exciting experience to run the race daily, "fixing our eyes on Jesus" (Heb. 12:1-2). It will be even more exciting when we experience that "upward calling" and Jesus returns to take us to heaven! Then we will stand before the *bema* to receive our rewards! It was this future prospect that motivated Paul, and it can also motivate us.

> *"All of us who are mature should take such a view of things. And if on some point you think differently, that too God will make clear to you. Only let us live up to what we have already attained"*
>
> *(Philippians 3:15-16).*

....

Applying God's Truth:

1. What "rules" of Christian living do you find hardest to obey on a regular basis?

2. How do you feel as you think about standing at the judgment seat of Christ to receive your rewards? Why?

3. What are three things you can do to ensure that you don't lose your rewards?

Read **Philippians 3:17-19**

Enemies of the Cross

....

The cross of Jesus Christ is the theme of the Bible, the heart of the Gospel, and the chief source of praise in heaven. The cross is the proof of God's love for sinners and God's hatred for sin. In what sense were the Judaizers the "enemies of the cross of Christ"? For one thing, the cross ended the Old Testament religion. By His death and resurrection, Jesus accomplished a "spiritual circumcision" that made ritual circumcision unnecessary (Col. 2:10-13). Everything the Judaizers advocated had been eliminated by the death of Christ on the cross.

Furthermore, everything that they lived for was condemned by the cross. Jesus had broken down the wall that stood between Jews and Gentiles, and the Judaizers were rebuilding that wall!

The true believer crucifies the flesh. He also crucifies the world. Yet, the Judaizers were minding "earthly things." It is the cross that is central in the life of the believer. He does not glory in men, in religion, or in his own achievements; he glories in the cross.

"As I have often told you before and now say again even with tears, many live as enemies of the cross of Christ"
(Philippians 3:18).

....

Applying God's Truth:

1. Do you know people you would consider "enemies of the cross of Christ"? How would you describe them?

2. What are your feelings toward people who are openly hostile to Christian teaching? Why?

3. How much thought have you put into the significance of the cross? Would you say you "glory" in the cross, or do you need to think some more about this subject?

Read **Philippians 3:20-21**

Dual Citizenship

....

The citizens of Philippi were privileged to be Roman citizens away from Rome. When a baby was born in Philippi, it was important that its name be registered on the legal records. When the lost sinner trusts Christ and becomes a citizen of heaven, his name is written in "the book of life" (Phil. 4:3).

Citizenship is important. When you travel to another country, it is essential that you have a passport that proves your citizenship. None of us wants to suffer the fate of Philip Nolan in the classic tale *The Man Without a Country.* Because he cursed the name of his country, Nolan was sentenced to live aboard ship and never again see his native land or even hear its name or news about its progress. For 56 years he was on an endless journey from ship to ship and sea to sea, and finally was buried at sea. He was a "man without a country."

The Christian's name is written in "the book of life," and this is what determines his final entrance into the heavenly country. When you confess Christ on earth, He confesses your name in heaven. Your name is written down in heaven and it stands written forever.

*"Our citizenship is in heaven. And we
eagerly await a Savior from there,
the Lord Jesus Christ"*
(Philippians 3:20).

....

Applying God's Truth:

1. Think of some groups and organizations to which
   you belong. What privileges do you have as a
   member of each group?

2. What privileges are you entitled to as a "citizen of
   heaven"?

3. What are your responsibilities as a citizen of
   heaven?

Read **Philippians 4:1-5**

The Antidote to Worry
....

If anybody had an excuse for worrying, it was the Apostle Paul. His beloved Christian friends at Philippi were disagreeing with one another, and he was not there to help them. We have no idea what Euodia and Syntyche were disputing about, but whatever it was, it was bringing division into the church. Along with the potential division at Philippi, Paul had to face division among the believers at Rome (Phil. 1:14-17). Added to these burdens was the possibility of his own death! Yes, Paul had a good excuse to worry — *but he did not!* Instead, he takes time to explain to us the secret of victory over worry.

The Old English root from which we get our word "worry" means "to strangle." If you have ever really worried, you know how it does strangle a person! In fact, worry has definite physical consequences: headaches, neck pains, ulcers, even back pains. Worry affects our thinking, our digestion, and even our coordination.

The antidote to worry is the secure mind: "The peace of God . . . will guard your hearts and your minds in Christ Jesus" (Phil. 4:7). When you have the secure

"Rejoice in the Lord always. I will say it again: Rejoice! Let your gentleness be evident to all. The Lord is near"
(Philippians 4:4-5).

....

mind, the peace of God guards you and the God of peace guides you! With that kind of protection — why worry?

Applying God's Truth:

1. What are three things you are worried about right now? If you begin to rejoice about other, more positive things, how do you think your worries would be affected?

2. Do you think it's really possible to rejoice always? Explain.

3. How might you reduce your amount of worrying in the future?

Read *Philippians 4:6-7*

Mind Guarding

....

Paul counsels us to take everything to God in prayer. "Don't worry about *anything,* but pray about *everything!*" is his admonition. We are prone to pray about the "big things" in life and forget to pray about the so-called "little things" — until they grow and become big things! Talking to God about *everything* that concerns us and Him is the first step toward victory over worry.

The result is that the "peace of God" guards the heart and the mind. You will remember that Paul is chained to a Roman soldier, guarded day and night. In like manner, "the peace of God" stands guard over the two areas that create worry — the heart (wrong feeling) and the mind (wrong thinking). When we give our hearts to Christ in salvation, we experience "peace with God" (Rom. 5:1); but the "peace of God" takes us a step further into His blessings. This does not mean the absence of trials on the outside, but it does mean a quiet confidence within, regardless of circumstances, people, or things.

*"Do not be anxious about anything, but
in everything, by prayer and petition,
with thanksgiving, present
your requests to God"*
(Philippians 4:6).

....

Applying God's Truth:

1. What are some "little things" in your life that
   concern you, yet that you may feel are too
   insignificant to pray about? (Whatever you think of,
   commit it to prayer and trust God to deal with the
   little things as well as the big ones.)

2. We tend to think of peace as an *inner* emotion. How
   do you feel when you envision God's peace as
   something that can protect you from outside
   influences?

3. What requests do you need to present to God
   today? What reasons do you have to offer
   thanksgiving today?

Read **Philippians 4:8-9**

The Right Balance

....

Paul balances four activities: "learned and received" and "heard and seen." It is one thing to *learn* a truth, but quite another to *receive* it inwardly and make it a part of our inner self. Facts in the head are not enough; we must also have truths in the heart. In Paul's ministry, he not only taught the Word but also lived it so that his listeners could see the truth in his life. Paul's experience ought to be our experience. We must learn the Word, receive it, hear it, and do it.

The peace of God is one test of whether or not we are in the will of God. If we are walking with the Lord, then the peace of God and the God of peace exercise their influence over our hearts. Whenever we disobey, we lose that peace and we know we have done something wrong.

Right praying, right thinking, and right living: these are the conditions for having the secure mind and victory over worry.

*"Whatever is true, whatever is noble, whatever
is right, whatever is pure, whatever is lovely,
whatever is admirable—if anything is excellent
or praiseworthy—think about such things.
Whatever you have learned or received or heard
from me, or seen in me—put it into practice"*
(Philippians 4:8-9).

....

Applying God's Truth:

1. Of learning, receiving, hearing, and seeing God's
   Word, which do you feel you do best? In which area
   do you need the most work?

2. What can you do to keep your thoughts true, pure,
   lovely, and so forth? How do you prevent less noble
   thoughts from sneaking in?

3. What are some things you can "think about" right
   now that will help purify your thought patterns?

Read **Philippians 4:10-12**

Learning Contentment

....

Contentment is not complacency, nor is it a false peace based on ignorance. The complacent believer is unconcerned about others, while the contented Christian wants to share his blessings. Contentment is not escape from the battle, but rather an abiding peace and confidence in the midst of the battle. Two words in verse 11 are vitally important—"learned" and "content."

The verb "learned" means "learned by experience." Paul's spiritual contentment was not something he had immediately after he was saved. He had to go through many difficult experiences of life in order to learn how to be content.

The word *content* actually means "contained." It is a description of the man whose resources are within him so that he does not have to depend on substitutes without. The Greek word means "self-sufficient" and was a favorite word of the Stoic philosophers. But the Christian is not sufficient in himself; he is sufficient in Christ. Because Christ lives within us, we are adequate for the demands of life.

"I have learned to be content whatever the circumstances. I know what it is to be in need, and I know what it is to have plenty"
(Philippians 4:11-12).

....

Applying God's Truth:

1. What are your major sources of discontentment? What causes you to be content?

2. Do you think you can learn to be content most of the time without undergoing suffering first? Why?

3. What would need to happen before you feel that you could be content—no matter *what* happens?

Read **Philippians 4:13-23**

Needs and Greeds

God has not promised to supply all our "greeds." When the child of God is in the will of God, serving for the glory of God, then he will have every need met. Hudson Taylor often said, "When God's work is done in God's way for God's glory, it will not lack for God's supply."

A young pastor came to a church that had been accustomed to raising its annual budget by means of suppers, bazaars, and the like. He told his officers he could not agree with their program. "Let's pray and ask God to meet every need," he suggested. "At the end of the month, pay all the bills and leave my salary till the last. If there isn't enough money for my salary, then I'm the one who suffers, and not the church. But I don't think anybody is going to suffer!" The officers were sure that both the pastor and the church would die, but such was not the case. Each month every bill was paid, and at the end of the year there was a surplus in the treasury for the first time in many years.

Contentment comes from adequate resources. Our resources are the providence of God, the power of God, and the promises of God. These resources made

> *"I can do everything through Him*
> *who gives me strength"*
> *(Philippians 4:13).*

....

Paul sufficient for every demand of life, and they can make us sufficient, too.

Applying God's Truth:

1. Are you careful to separate your needs from your "greeds"? Can you think of anything you've been praying for that may not be a legitimate need?

2. Can you think of anything you've been wanting to ask God for, yet are hesitant because it seems like too great a request? Based on today's verse, are you ready now to ask for it?

3. Can you think of ways that God might use *you* to supply someone else's need?